Abnormal Repetitive Behaviors

Abnormal Repetitive Behaviors

poems

LESLIE HEYWOOD

RED HEN PRESS | PASADENA, CA

Book layout by Latina Vidolova

Library of Congress Cataloging-in-Publication Data

Names: Heywood, Leslie, author.
Title: Abnormal repetitive behaviors / Leslie Heywood.
Description: First edition. | Pasadena, CA : Red Hen Press, [2016]
Identifiers: LCCN 2015050378 | ISBN 9781597097307 (paperback)
Subjects: | BISAC: POETRY / General.
Classification: LCC PS3558.E93 A6 2016 | DDC 811/.54—dc23
LC record available at http://lccn.loc.gov/2015050378

The National Endowment for the Arts, the Los Angeles County Arts Commission, the
Los Angeles Department of Cultural Affairs, the Dwight Stuart Youth Fund, the Pasade-
na Arts & Cultural Commission and the City of Pasadena Cultural Affairs Division, Sony
Pictures Entertainment, and Ahmanson Foundation partially support Red Hen Press.

First Edition
Published by Red Hen Press
www.redhen.org

For my father, John Sephton Heywood, 1936–2014

CONTENTS

II

III

"She had learned, in her life, that time lived inside you. You are time, you breathe time. When she'd been young, she'd had an insatiable hunger for more of it, though she hadn't understood why. Now she held inside her a cacophony of times and lately it drowned out the world . . . making way for the boy inside to run along before her. It could be hard to choose the time outside over the time within."

—Almondine (the dog's) perspective,
in *The Story of Edgar Sawtelle*

Prologue

Abnormal Repetitive Behaviors

Or "stereotypies," as animal behavioral
Researchers sometimes call them, are seen
Especially in research animals who live
Their lives in tiny cages, or who live
In larger cages in zoos, anywhere there is
A sense of conflict and panic and feeling trapped.

You've seen it happen, so many versions of Rilke's
Panther pacing back and forth, back and forth,
Within the tight cube of a zoo cage; in the wolf
Who, even in an enclosure six backyards long,
Wears the same path across the same stones
Across the same log, even across a human's leg

If it happens to protrude across her path.
Beyond the bars, or whatever takes
The place of bars, *no world*.
But it isn't only animals who do this.
There's a YouTube video going around
Showing a sobbing autistic teenager.

He stands backed against a wall and every
Fifteen seconds or so pounds his fists into his forehead.
His sobs are moans and so lost I can't help but flinch,
But then on the left side of the camera
In leaps a dog, a black lab, who nuzzles

Under the boy's arms and keeps nuzzling
Even as the boy tries to push him away
But the dog brings his body right up against

The boy, who manages to hit himself smack
In the forehead just one more time but then
Gives up, falls to his knees with his arms

Around the dog, and the dog holds him up,
And this seems to make the boy go steady
So that for a while more he sobs, then stops,
Just stops and holds the dog, so yes, humans
Have sterotypies, too, because we have the same
Animal brains, same place in the brainstem
Where the basics get torn or brought forth
By all the creatures around us:
Seeking caring panic fear anger lust love play,
Torn so one or more of them just
Doesn't get expressed right. It's not only people
With autism. I am not autistic
Yet how often I stand in exactly the same

Position as that sobbing boy, sobbing
In just the same way, a cry stuck between
Growling and the most bereft sense of loss,
Sobbing until I can't breathe and it's always
Right about this point I start pounding my fists
Into my forehead, the dull thud like a kayak

Bumping up against a wooden dock.
If I am that boy in the video, then how
Many of the rest of us? So human, so animal
Experience most often comes to this: the dull
Thump, the hollow sob. And, if care still exists,
Can still reach beyond our panic—the calming nuzzle.

I

Night Ranger (Don't Tell Me You Love Me)

It is four decades later but my body
Behaves as if it does not know this,
As if everything now is the same
As it was then and it is on guard,
This body, on guard before it thinks,
On guard before it sees, and when it sees
Everything comes flooding back
Through that exact screen:
It is always night, it is always quiet
But I am waiting for noise,
Noise of a specific kind
And yet a lot of other noises
Resemble it, making my heart
Start to pound: the neighbor's kids,
Their voices all in shriek. The slightest
Shift in tone in a loved one's voice.
The sound of heavy equipment
Moving anywhere along the street.
Something as simple as a blue jay's cry.

These sounds meld into
My father's voice forty years ago,
Heading into night. He's been
Quiet for awhile and I know that
That's where the trouble is,
And soon the thin scarf of silence
Will be torn by these clipped words
So full of heat, always *death* and *whore*
And *why is anyone even alive* until the heat
Builds and the words break free, louder,

So much louder and I can't hear what they say
They are the crash of huge waves
At the most dangerous beach and they
Sweep me up, throw me down, drowning
In the way oxygen flees from my chest
Shuts down so there isn't any movement
In my lungs and up and up until the words stop
And then there is touch but somehow
This is better *come on, come on, get up on your feet*
Let's see if you've learned yet to fight
And there is a hand around my arm
Like the grip of a backhoe digging in
To bring something up and I stumble
At first but this is better, I can push,
I can hit, I can use the top of my head
As a battering ram and this happened so long
Ago I just don't care anymore just someone
Else's sordid story except I still sit there
Ear turned to the world
Expecting this.

Velvet Collars, Acid Rain

In the 1970s Northeastern United States,
Acid rain started killing the fish in the lakes,
Eating away at all the trees, the gathering
Of years of sulfur dioxide and nitrogen oxide
From burning fossil fuels like coal,
The trout belly-up in the Adirondack lakes
Where my father worked trying to save them:
The young of most species are more sensitive
To environmental conditions than adults
And I remember those fish, white bellies
Floating, trunks of trees stripped, the sick
Yellow leaves.

Humans destroy everything my father
Said, his life destroyed at thirteen: a shot
From his father's rifle through his mother's
Left breast, a shot by his father's own hand
Into his own left temple. Or maybe
It was destroyed earlier than this:

He told my mother his mother was crazy,
Chaining him to the piano
For six a.m. practice when the light first broke,
Not letting him speak to his father—

I have my doubts. His mother's name
Was Annie. Unlike so many women
In the 1930s and 40s
She had a college degree. She loved
Beautiful things. She wanted my father

To live beauty, dressing him
In *Little Lord Fauntleroy* suits:
Long velvet collars spilling over tweed blazers
And matching knee-length trousers,
Thick shiny patent-leather boots.

She wanted him to be a concert pianist,
And I know she could see herself
Rising out of Mechanicville (that cold
And grimy northeastern railroad town,
Its houses grim with collapsing porches
Limned with black coal dust and flaking
Paint) with each note my father played,
Up out of her body away from her trapped
Days with no beauty to redeem them even
Slightly, smokestacks belching coal
So thick it would settle on the silk shawl
She tried to keep clean,

The other women pushing the seams
Of their rough woolen floor length skirts,
Their faces set so it seemed
There was no way to pull the bones
Or the muscles that leveraged them
Into anything resembling a smile. The way
Their mouths pressed down, their skin
All gray, as if all light had fled.

My father was late in Annie's life,
His brother Robert thirteen years older

With the dead brother, Harold, in between.
If my father was conceived to reinvigorate
A ghost he did a good job of it,
For when his parents met their violent end,
I can only imagine what died in him. Was it beauty,
Was it grace his mother gave him, his piano
Playing the notes of this strange dirge
Like a silk scarf riven, its fabric
Regurgitating threads, some small remnant
Of a beauty more whole? Musical notes
Like a parachutist dropped
From the sky, my father in his tweed suits
Velvet bow around the throat, playing,
Playing, head down,

Hopscotching through years, fingers
So sure of themselves they seemed
To give off sparks through his tears
That fell on the piano keys the one time
My mother heard him play—

I never stopped loving my father,
And she didn't either, too much rage
In her voice all those years later
When I called to ask if she would help
Pay his cremation expenses
Or if we should let my father's body
Revert back to the state, the fund
For indigents, for the bodies of those
With none to claim them.

My Father's Shoulders

I am the daughter who followed you around
Like I was the earth tracking your sun,
How tall you were, the great wall of your back
Like you could hold me and all the rest
Of the world overhead. You got down
On the floor with me, hiding your head
Under your arms on the rug made of skin
From the bear you shot, your head resting
By his head, patient while I shrieked and climbed.
What a mountain you were, my feet planted
In your shoulder grooves while I gurgle
To my mother, *look at me!*
And thinking about it now I know
A daughter's supposed to run and hide behind
Her mother's knees when a stranger addresses her
Or a growling dog draws near
But I never did for there was always
You instead, the picture of us
Outside the Altamont State Fair when I was ten,
Our arms folded across our chests in exactly
The same way, our chins angled back
While we look down on shrieks of people
Passing round us on Ferris wheels
While we stand back, two glowering statues
Carved from wood. I studied you,
The way you walked with shoulders back,
Hips straight with steps that devoured space,
The daughter who never grew out of it: this, my love
For you as fierce as that snarling bear's stuffed head.

He Didn't

The wind comes up, trees shift.
If it happens to blow hard enough,
Or fast enough, a branch
Might bring down a power line, smash
Through a porch, crush the neighbor's
Swing. Trees rooted for years—the giant oak,
Slim Japanese maple—might tear
From the ground. The wind, the shrieks,
Then quiet, sun. Disaster in quietest corners,
Black teens shot by police officers
For walking down the street. Or a white girl
Is drunk and slips her hand on her steering wheel,
Her Chevy Tahoe tilting into a mother's
Brand new Jeep. We are insane
To be unafraid, and yet we must be. Last April,
A call out of nowhere in the afternoon
Just before work, my father,
Whom I haven't seen in years,
Is dead. It was a Wednesday. I had office
Hours, talked to students, did not cry
Until much later. Shreds of a world,
A blanket skin around us. It was his landlord
Who brought him to the hospital where he died.
There was a nurse there, the landlord told me,
He didn't die alone. The wind comes up.
The wind comes up. The trees shift.

Said There Was Trouble

My second grade bedroom at the top of the stairs
Was painted robin's egg blue as if to fend off
The dark around us like some dirge the earth
Groaned up: blizzards, subzero, the woodstove
In the basement my father fed coal like he fed
Himself Budweiser in those awful creaking cans,

The metal collapsing like scaffolding
Each time he'd crunch an empty in his fist,
His fist like his father's clenched tight
On a shotgun in October 1949, clenching, unclenching,
Until he straightened out his shoulders and took aim,
My grandmother crumpling like paper

From a bullet that entered her shoulder,
Exited her left breast and buried itself
In the living room wall that night my father
Was thirteen, asleep in his own room
That could only have been white,
Gray charcoal army blanket folded

At the bottom of his bed and I know
Just what he must have felt like
When that shot that divided the first part
Of his life from all the rest woke him,
Threw him forward as he crept to see
The bodies, for there were two shots,

The *Albany Register* said, and his father
Called his brother,

Said *there's been a little trouble*
And you'd better come up to the house,
Then shot himself, my father there to find them
Long before his uncle ever came,
Dividing one part of his life from the rest

The way my shelves of Breyer
Horse statues stood still
Against my bedroom wall, silent,
Presiding over everything
That went on beneath them
Like some merciless judges,
Or those spinning sisters Fates.

What I Took from My Father's House the Weekend after He Died

A metal baseball bat we used for Wiffle ball.
An old duffel bag I remembered.
A binder from a job, "Arizona Sonora Desert Museum
Comprehensive Plan" on front. A half-empty
Jar of aspirin from his kitchen.
Two off-white washcloths with their edges
Frayed. A picture of a polar bear.
A picture of mountains in Montana.
A laminated tag from an airline bag,
"John Heywood, Executive Director,
Montana Tech Foundation." A plaque,
"First Place Men, 55-Over, Discovery
Basin Adult Ski Raves 1989."
A red carabineer.

A stack of CDs:
Johnny Cash. Rachmaninoff *Preludes*.
Shostakovich. Stravinsky. George Winston.
Fleetwood Mac. Roger Whittaker. Prokofiev.
Ravel. Grieg. A stack of books:
Atlas Shrugged. A Farewell to Arms.
Medicare and You 2013. Webster's New
Collegiate Dictionary. The Audubon Society
Guide to Birds of North America.
His tan wool Carhartt hat. Gray
Duluth Trading Company fleece gloves.
A pint-sized mason jar filled with tiny
Gray and white stones. A gargoyle,
Arms clasped around its knees.
A used roll of silver Scotch duct tape.
A copper-plated birdfeeder.

A small red container
Of Pro-Shot all-weather oil. A
Picture of my father with his
Golden retrievers, his long
White beard like Santa Claus
Or Rip Van Winkle. A bowl carved
From a species of Chinese fir,
Shan Mu. A documentary-style painting,
"Sharing the Habitat," of mallard ducks
and Canadian geese in flight over a lake.
An Olan Mills portrait of my family
From the 1970s, my father, my mother,
My sister and I all dressed in maroon, our
Irish setter and Samoyed in front of us.
An Olan Mills portrait of my sister and I,
On which I had written, "I love you. Merry Christmas.
Leslie," and my sister had written, "Merry Christmas
To my Daddy, Love Heidi." I have a gap between
My teeth. We're wearing matching pink shirts.
A business picture in a cellophane wrapper of my father
In a black suit and tie, "Jon Wolf Photography,
Tucson, Arizona, 1986."

His coffee pot. His blue enamel camp bowl
And plate from the drainboard.
The yellowest wineglass in a display case of many.
The last fork, knife, and spoon he had set out to dry.
A corkscrew. Some of his ashes in an Inca clay pot.
A weather thermometer sitting on his desk.
Some orange-handled scissors. A Grundig

Emergency alert radio. A metal belt buckle
With a grizzly. A Stanley Power Lock sixteen foot
Measuring tape. Datebooks from 2012 and 2013
Filled with exact lists of numbers, $74.16, $40.88,
And the dates of haircuts, house cleanings, physical
Therapy appointments. A manila folder,
My name and address on it, though he hadn't
Talked to me for years. Edgar Allen Poe postage
Stamps. A list of phone numbers, names
I don't know. A stapler, and staples.
A Hallmark Christmas ornament of the Grinch.
His Rolodex, a Timex Expedition watch. A Levenger
Leather notepad cover. Diplomas from Middlebury College
And Northwood Prep School, Lake Placid, New York, fifteen miles
From where he ended up living the rest of his life.

A prescription
For forearm crutches due to leg
Edema and osteoarthritis.
Leather billfold with empty index cards.
A pair of wire-rimmed glasses.
Bookmarks from Ducks Unlimited,
Wheels and Water Safety, and the
World Wildlife Fund, held together
With a paper clip. A Christmas card I sent
In 2006. Prescriptions for Propoxyphene and Lisinopril.
An index card with a quote from Dryden handwritten
On one side, "But What Has Been Has Been, and I Have Had
My Hour," and Dylan Thomas's "Do Not Go Gentle Into that Good
Night, Old Age Should Burn and Rave at Close of Day, Rage,

Rage Against the Dying of the Light" on the other. A list of channel
Numbers for the sports stations. His last grocery list:
Nature Valley Honey Breakfast Biscuits. Butter.
Antipasto. Two Drumsticks. Two Del Monte
Fruit Naturals. Two Campbells' Beef Bowls. One
Medium Club Soda. The Wild America calendars
From his wall. Gempler's Outdoor Workwear 2014 March
Catalogue. A Kershaw wilderness knife. A white candle.
A plastic dinosaur. Some leather shoelaces.
A magnifying glass. The pencil from his desk.

LACK OF RUNNING WATER
IN THE WEST

It was not unusual in our house
For any of us to say *you are such*
A fucking idiot or *look how ugly*
You are, you're disgusting or
The human race is a cancer
On the planet or my father,
Addressing the dog, saying
Dogs are much better than people,
You know (something I still say
To this day).

It was not unusual in our house
For the Christmas tree to fly
Out the window, or for my father,
In black-out moments, to throw
His hand-carved loons and Canadian
Geese into the fireplace, watch
Them burn, and then poke
Through the ashes in the morning,
Head tilted to the side, wondering
How they had gotten there.

It was not unusual in our house
For me to fight with my father
When I was seven, learning how
To dodge, and twist, and hit
At just the right moment
When his balance was off,
Nor was it unusual for my mother

To pull me in front of her body when I was five,
A shield between her and my father's fists.

It was not unusual to get up
In the morning and go into the kitchen
Looking for Wheaties and find a set
Of shattered dishes, a rainbow of glass
Paving a yellow brick road,
Not unusual to hear about
The lack of running water in the West
And how we were all doomed
(this was the 1970s, and forty years later,
Little towns in California run dry, one by one),
By this, his booming voice,
The crunch of Budweiser cans,
The battle siege one night at a time,
But in the morning,
Nothing, pure lack of sound,
Held breath.

Mythology

It was not meant to be this way,
My sister cowering inside of her room,
Never poking her head out until morning
When all had been leveled, the ruins
Given their time to smolder out, the hiss
And pop of words like wood fragments
From a rising fire from which she could
Only catch those that exploded the furthest,
The sparks that fell outside the protective screen:
Bitch die horrible ugly come to nothing
And she didn't know even who the words
Were for, just that she had to stay
Out of their way and she did, her room
A strong boat bumping on the other side
Of the stormiest sea where the monsters
Lived like something out of the legends
Of ancient Greece: our father, blown
Up three dimensions with his anger,
A whirl of fist inarticulate at this point
Like the raving Ajax; me, a tiny Odysseus,
Seven-year-old limbs bunched tight
And running at him head first,
Or landing light punches before dashing
Away, drawing him further away from my mother,
Andromeda chained by the edge of the sea held
By the surreality of all this, the fire of words
And the ocean that swallowed us,
Spat us out to live normal lives
And then come back to fight
This fight, always this same fight.

HEART RATE VARIABILITY

When I move fast my heart rate shoots up
To a speed where many other
Hearts would stop, 180, maybe, but mine
Just sticks there through an hour or three
Of training and even when I slow back down
It hovers for a long time before settling
Into slow-mode, anti-siege. My coaches
Could make no sense of this but since it helped
They weren't concerned and I wasn't
Either: my magic heart, my trick organ
That could behave as if fighting for its life
For such long intervals of time.
The pieces came together long after
I ran races for trophies and scholarships and times:
Individuals reporting greater frequency
And duration of daily worry have reduced
Heart rate variability as if my tendency
To sit and wait for the tone in someone's voice
To shift (and bring me out, fists swinging),
Has changed the shape and tone in the muscle
Of the heart itself and its regulating engine:
Stay on. Danger ahead. All speed.

APOCRYPHA

Some moments stay with us
Like a flashbulb that catches
That instant in your mind for good:
Time stops then, some part of you
Is always frozen there, you live
There and not your current life
No matter how different that is.

One of these for me is a radio
Thrown at my mother's head,
But since she was holding me
In front of her it hit me
Instead, just a little bit,
The sharp corner of its wooden
Casing catching me just above
My elbow, a dull thud pressing
The skin so it looked like
I had a dent in my arm for two weeks.

I was five and can't remember
Anything else, what might have happened
That year, what kindergarten felt like,
What books I read, what games
I liked to play. I remember
Looking at the dent near my elbow
As if I were looking at some other kid, thinking
It was interesting the skin didn't
Puff back out.

I had no way of knowing
How long I would be trapped here
How many decades it would take
To dig back out, to feel
My elbow existing anywhere
But that living room with its double-bluestone
Fireplace, the rocks that held it up
Suddenly part of my skin.

Supplies

In my remembered childhood
It is always winter, we are always
Losing power and the snow is finding
A way to sweep underneath
The specially insulated storm doors
The lead from the living room
Onto the redwood deck, the storm
Door in front of which my sleeping bag
Lies in the shape of a green frog
With black and white googly
Felt eyes that I use for a pillow
As I climb into his mouth and wake
With snow in my hair, wake
And the pipes are frozen
And the dogs pace about sensing
Something is wrong for my father
Is angry, he needs to fix this
So he can get back to his office
With its gleaming black desk
With its mementos of the University
For which he raises money stacked
In cabinets of the finest crafted ash
And he always brings me home
Writing pads and pencils
With the university insignia inscribed
And I love those pencils,
Drawing pictures of dragons
I stuff in my backpack
With frozen hands, always winter,
Only sunlight in late afternoon

So weak you can't feel it,
Always winter and my father
Brings me pencils
And I am grateful for this.

RAGGEDY ANNE

Halloween when I was six, my sister three,
She got to be Raggedy Andy and I didn't,
Stuck, at my mother's insistence, with Raggedy Anne,
As if at six it was time for me to stop messing around
With pretending to be a boy, first grade
Too late for such games:

No more riding the red and black Scorpion
Snowmobile behind my father, our thick black
Snowsuits a quilt against the two-hundred-year-old
Whispers of the pines, our twin aviator shades
Dark mirrors on which the reflection of the other lived,
My tough nut of a body the toy version of his
His same squared off shoulders and slate blue eyes,
No more following him out with my toy chainsaw
Pretending to carve that massive oak like the biting teeth
Of his, no more sitting together on the cut stump
Listening to wind and the calls of the nuthatches
Between the trees.

Halloween when I was six, he'd stopped
Taking me with him to the workshop behind Howard Hurley's
Place where they'd tell stories about what it might be like
To live out west while they'd smoke Winston-Salems,
Drink Budweiser beer, my father always sneaking me
A sip, though he didn't whenever my mother appeared,
My mother who gave me
Raggedy Anne in her dreaded dresses
And girl pigtails like shark skin
Slid over my face, that fierce,
That forced, that strange.

WIDOW'S PEAK

My father is
The cold wind of a January freeze,
A hawk's dented feather
On bluestone shale,
A hand, its knuckles thickened,
Face with blood just under the skin,

Hair that went suddenly gray,
A widow's peak for light,
Muscles clumped like sacked coal,
That heavy, shoulders dragged forward
When he sits, the light that is gone
When he slips,

Eyes that measure you up
Gauging the right time, burned snowmobile oil,
Old cans of gasoline, the old scratchy wool
Of a Pendleton shirt, Maine trapper's boots
From L.L.Bean, thick leather gloves
With pocks and grit.

My father is a snowstorm
That drives so hard
The flakes make it underneath
The storm doors, he is the gas shortages
Of the 1970s, his green Jeep CJ-7
With its canvas top

Cracking in the wind,
He is the voice missed

At Christmas, a mailbox
Always empty, a dot on a map
That showed where he lived
Where I never made it out
Until he died.

SNOW GLOBE

Saturday afternoon at our house is the time before,
Time before darkness, time before flames from the fireplace,
Quiet like breath, held there, paused,
Hovering, waiting, as if the four of us
And our two dogs were suspended
At the top of a snow globe, not the stationary figures
That the flakes swirl around but the flakes themselves,
Caught in that instant between
When you turn the globe upside down and shake,
And the moment after it's been righted
And the flakes are paused, about to swirl,
Begin their fall. And we are the creatures
In miniature like this, looked at
From so far away:

An interesting occasion. A social worker's
Case, all the different therapists who tried
To change our lives and never could, a roar
No talk can cure.

The birch outside the window
Has slender branches
The wind and snow pin back:
They also hover, they also wait.
They wait and see if the snow will be
A burden here, enough to make them snap,

And when it does, the sound
Is like a pistol shot so definite
In its release: this, my father's voice,

Words lost in the roar then more definite
Still, his foot against the husky's ribs,
The husky's cry. My father's fist
Through the wall, my face
The shock that he had missed.

The Last Toyota Pickup

The last Toyota pickup my father owned,
Like all the other versions, was white,
Tailgate down and filled lengthwise
With half-sawn logs, their trunks
Rough-cut above Montana plates. A silver
Heavy-duty toolbox
Sits behind them, and on it sits Chula,
My father's Airedale terrier, the one he got
When my last dog from childhood passed away.
Because I saw him so little I didn't know her
Well but there she sits, his closest companion
For fifteen years, ears forward in contentment
Lost among the curls of her unclipped fur.
By the truck sits more half-cut logs
Piled sideways and windshield-height high,
Bark rough-shot through with sun,
Montana prairie grass spilling over the tires.

I found this picture
Alone in an envelope in a pile of date books
And check stubs and physical therapy
Receipts stored in the corner
Of my father's desk on a Friday morning
The week after he died.

I was looking for a letter he'd said
He would write the last time
I talked to him two summers before
But there was nothing but empty
Lined notepads and receipts

From the small-town library
Across the street. That he
Should leave without words is no surprise
Since there were never many.
That sequence of Jeeps and pickups
Fitted out to haul wood, some
Space for a dog beside them
Were reliable, the one thing
Repeated, one thing
I could trust:
A dog with sun on her fur.
A stack of half-sawn logs.
A prairie grass.
Silence.

II

Sit

Imagine a tree tipped forward,
A Japanese maple, roots letting go.
Some wind
Has taken it out.

Imagine that you planted it there
Fifteen years before
Dark crimson leaf tips
Slim gray trunk
Some assurance
Of a future
Some assurance
This one will not leave you
This one will stay in place.

And yet a bad wind blows
And now the roots stack stiff
From the ground like rakes
And the one you planted it with
Left years ago
And though there have been others
Who came to sit
In exactly that place

You remember his hands
When he tucked the roots in,
His fingertips tamping down dirt
Into each precious place.

Too Little, Too Much

Places I've lived: East Berne,
New York; Parker, Colorado;
Tucson, Arizona; Laguna Beach,
California; Vestal, New York,
These places as far apart
As the country's stretch. Trees
In the Northeast, so dense
And green, the oaks, the maples,
Hemlocks, birch. The other side
Is desert: cholla, mesquite.

The one is too much,
Rain for days and everything
Wet, mushrooms growing
On the logs outside, lichens
Covering the pipes, weeds
That pop up three for each
You pull. The other too much sun and dust,
Water riven from your skin
The moment you step off the plane,
Everything bone, bone, cactus rib,
Collapsed red water sack
On top of the prickly pear.

Too many things growing, not enough.
Rivers flooding one place, groundwater
Evaporating in the other. Too little, too much.
Too little, too much, Sonoran collared lizards
Scurrying across soil so bleached
It isn't dirt or even sand, northern redback

Salamanders emerging in threes
From underneath last fall's leaves,
That eastern canopy that lives and dies
Within six months, and the West,
Nothing ever changing, just open sky
And dust and dust and dust.

STATE LINE

After you cross the Mississippi heading west
You see the sky change from a thick green blanket
Upheld by trunks to an eye socket hollow.
When I was ten, I thought those
Open spaces were the most frightening things
I'd ever seen. Not ready to trade sycamore and oak
For acacia and scrub pine, what I knew was that
I was leaving everything I knew behind.

The year before that the doctors
Weren't sure after the liver damage
How much longer my father had to live
But he laughed it off and carried on
Like nothing happened, except he was fed up
With these close-up trees and said
We'd travel west, where the scrub jay
Was welcome and pack rats found water
In the red meat cactus fruits.
It's not like anything had really changed,
From east to west, west to east, he outlived

Those names anyone
Saw fit to give: *Depressive. Alcoholic.*
Spouse abuser, unchangeable as drops of rain,
What remains when monsoons
Have exhausted themselves and left.

Rear Axle

That time, years ago, driving west,
My sister rode in the U-Haul
Between my mother and father
Up ahead, her nine-year-old head
With its cover of curls
Motionless between them.

I rode in the back of our old Jeep CJ-7,
Attached to the U-Haul by a hitch,
Me and our dogs at the time,
An Irish setter and a Siberian husky
With one blue eye, one brown.

They flanked either side of me
Like fur-covered bookends as we drowsed
In the Jeep's back seat, driving cross-country
From upstate New York to the small
Colorado suburb where soon we would live.

The dogs and I drowsed our way
Across seven states, until the three of us
Sat up straight: a creak from the trailer hitch,
Then a lurch and a thud as we sprang
Backwards and landed by the side
Of the I-66, the U-Haul disappearing
Forward without us attached, now crossing
The horizon line, the dogs whining,

My hands in their fur, my head resting
On their flanks where we sat
The two hours it took my family
To make it back and claim us.

White Paint

The heat that Tucson May was fierce,
Rising from the desert floor in waves,
Air thick with the dust from the exhaust
Of trucks, the roar of planes from
The Air Force base where retired planes
Sat baking in the sun, more ghostly each
Year as if heat breaks them down
Molecule by molecule and no one sees
Until the steel gives in. We were
So young, it seemed everything was at stake,
As if each breath depended on what
We did next and that day we met
At "A" Mountain, that sentinel peak
To the south of downtown where each year
Some group of civically minded students
Heads out on a Saturday morning
Before the sun comes up
To rebleach the "A" with white paint.

People came to the mountain
For all kinds of reasons: to park
Their cars and watch the lights, to hike
Before daybreak, to sit and drink Jim Beam,
And you have none of the history of this place,
Don't know the hypodermic needles left between rocks,
Don't know the trail smooth as a snake's back
Among the jumping cholla, the thousand things
With needles, so I guide you across it,
Not up the hill but down the trail
Snaking shale into a cave, an improbable

Place made partly of cement from some
Long washed-out bridge, partly a space
Someone had dug under the chollas
And propped up with rocks underneath.

Blue paint for graffiti, old condoms
And coke cans pushed down
By the sun's rising up by degrees
And you and I in our twenties
Fierce against the rocks
Like those Air Force planes
All roar to fly
Before their life is spent.

Fire Breathing

I'm fifteen and every day after school
I go to the high school track, its
Black tar melting and smelling of oil
In the Arizona sun, the fourth-inch
Metal spikes of my racing shoes
Sticking into the surface so that
Instead of speeding me up, my feet
Get stuck there for a fraction
Of a second, fractions add up
But we run on anyway, noting just how
High our body temperatures spike
Running through a hundred and five
Degrees. *My little tomato-faced*
Runner, my coach always calls me
And running like this, face
Hot as the pavement and blood
Pounding harder than track spikes
Through my head it gets difficult
To breathe and some survival impulse
Starts saying stop just stop now stop
And I'm afraid if I don't stop
There won't be any oxygen left
And I am scared but don't stop
Because the boys that I train with will laugh
And tell me girls are weak and the coach will laugh
And say the same thing and on the inside
Of my eye there's this picture
I can't get out where I'm being pushed
Down the stairs and can't get up
Because I am not weak,

Because I need to stand up
Run faster than the voices
No one else hears because if I don't
I'll fade away behind them,
My body disappearing in the heat.

SWITCHBACK

Outside Tucson, Arizona, the General
Hitchcock Highway splits
Like a fist along the mountain,
Jumbling into a set of knots
along each switchback, each curve
another thousand feet high.
Otherwise known as the Mount
Lemmon Highway, Arizona Forest
Highway 39, or the Sky Island Scenic Byway,

Each ascending shift of trees is an island
Of forest in a desert sea, so that it
Starts with saguaros and chollas
Up through stands of juniper
And pinyon pine until there is the stand of aspens
Bending into firs twenty-seven miles above,
Hovering over the clouds. I've biked up
That road and run it, sometimes in sections
And once the whole way, the Mount Lemmon
Marathon, where they ran out of water and Gatorade
At all the aid stations between miles sixteen
And twenty-three, and the few people
Who live there came out
In the Toyota pickups and their Ford F-150s
And gave us water dipped from Coleman coolers
Which some of us drank and some of us
Just splashed across our faces. You and I

Drove up that highway, too, all those crazy
High school summers we couldn't take

The sun and you had an old 1955 T-bird
You got from your grandfather, the car that always
Lost its brakes on steep declines
So that you got us down the mountain
One switchback at a time
By intermittent use of the emergency brake
So it was like we were flying, coasting by
Some improbability we'd never face
Until we landed all those years later
No brake to hold us into place.

YELLOW

If the sun still rises wherever you go,
All the same its color is different,
From tongue-thick mustard to daffodil thin,
The particulates in the air that day
A charcoal rubbed over its sheen.
There were days in that Tucson desert when
Its heat beat white and no yellow at all
Just headache and noise and I never
Could have borne this without you,
You who made sense only in the scratches
Of trails in some cactus-studded park
Outside town, so large you were
Against the high-noon silence, cicadas hushed,
Where nothing survives except heat.

Spotlight

There are twenty or so at the party
I organized in the desert
Where the sun in October is still bright,
Warm enough that even at seven at night
My daughters splash in the pool, their voices
Mixed with boys' voices, English and Spanish
Phrases filling the night, the sons
Of my old friend, and of the twenty

There are five of us here in the kitchen,
The boys with cerveza and me with tequila
Although instead of boys
They are middle-aged men,
And one of them, our coach,
Older still, and we are gathered here
Like spotted moths drawn to the overhead
Light, its wings a twitched beat

To the sound of our words,
Our laughter, more than twenty years
Since any of us have seen each other
And here we are drawn together
In a circle so tight there's no room
For anyone else, for our families,
Who drift in and out smiling at us
And our antics, our quick-fitted words:

Do you remember the time when, and *how is Ray*
And *whatever happened to Chris*
And suddenly Dave breaks out the letter

"A" jacket, old nylon, deep green,
And stiffer with years than even us.
This he says *do you remember I wanted this*
Top seven jacket so badly my first year on the team
And you, Victor, who had it, and you, Leslie

The only girl who ever did, how I wanted to be fast
The way you all were and all of us smile
The ghost of those years under our faces
So different from what we looked like then
But we are here as if not a single year
Has intervened, as if our feet on the road
Coiling the miles like a rattlesnake
Will always bind us to each other, call us home.

Dragon's Breath

I never wanted to come from a town
Where the identical Colonial or Victorian
Houses were just larger in some
Neighborhoods but are basically
The same thing, moss from too much
Rain spotting everyone's roof,
The sky always gray, each yard
With its own form of drainage
Problem, gutters clogged, pipes askew,
The people with their terrible hair,
Women with short perms and men
With nothing resembling a style
At all, their clothes as nondescript
As the houses: flower prints
For the women and men all in khakis
Or something worse, this town
Like a dragon's breath of ugliness
Exhaled upon the ground
And the people moving like shadows,
Their faces set, looking not right
Or not left making the turn onto
The Parkway in their years old Ford
Mini-vans with a car deodorizer
Hanging from the front mirror swaying
With the curve. The faces
Never lift. There is no hope here,
As if the rain, the snow in winter,
The way IBM and other businesses
Long gone had all come to live inside
Them, each day one Sisyphus step
Into the next, into the grave.

LIGHT GREEN OF NEW LEAVES GATHERS

Light green of new leaves gathers
Like an inheld breath, sky thick
With rain, trunks dark with wet,
A stillness where we sit and wait.
Last September 8, my birthday,

The sky was filled with rage
And dumped three feet of water within sixteen hours
That the arms of the land could not withstand. Water
Flowed into basements,
Up to the entry doors at Walmart

Where workers scurried
To set sandbags
To keep it at bay, slabs of meat
Rotting in the freezers
When the power went.

We drove to where the waterline
Made the strip-mall parking lot
Into a beach, the tops of abandoned cars
Rounded like dolphin backs flashing to the surface
Just before the dive down.

My friend Joe, evacuated from his house,
Spoke a grim oratory at the edge of the waters,
My girls silent, holding onto my hands
As all around us, people drove to the edge
Of the water and stood still.

Eight months later the rain gathers
In growing puddles in the yard and the hopeful leaves
Seem strange. We got the last of the mud from the basement
Just last week, and what is left to us
Is the legacy of our own selfishness, shame.

Five Years In

Last night I drove to the place
By the signal tower, the only space
Clear at this mountaintop thick with oaks
And tamarack pines, and pulled the car
Into this clearing to think.

There were the usual stars, the usual
Lights from the city on the hills
Looking down, and off to the side
The wild turkeys scuffled as they picked
Through the milkweed seeds.

My husband and children were safe
Home in bed about a mile down
The hill, my brain full of them,
But when I looked out across
The seeds of light I wondered
Which was yours, what difference
It might blink among the indistinguishable
Strings, and though I thought it might
Be the bluer one off to the right,
I knew it was only a guess.

I sat so still for a time
The deer drew near, the engine
Clicked itself to sleep. Starlight,
Starbright, each star I see tonight
Is you, but among those stars
We don't live.

St. Francis

I imagine St. Francis speaking to me,
Saying *bless you, my child, for you*
Have always seen your dogs as kin
While those from your own species
Are something alien and strange.

Walking the dogs after the snowstorm
They are crazy for release, the Akitas
Sticking their square bear heads
Into drifts, light beginning to fail
So the snow is like a silencer

Among the canopy of trees, the hush
Comes down to shape
The world anew and the dogs
Seem to take it like this, the narrowed streets,
The mailboxes peeking out of banks

The snow a dust of crunch
Underneath their feet. Tails up,
Paws down, what lies beneath
Is the network of memories
Of all the years they've walked here:

The spot where the Irish terrier
Rushes at them, tethered to the concrete block
She drags behind her, the house on the corner
Where the matching black Labs pace the length
Of their fence, or the spot from a deck

Where the golden Lab barks down at them,
His voice caught between *this is mine*
And *please don't come up here.* They look
For the dog that belongs to each yard
Even when they are not out,

The smells they've left buried everywhere
Beneath this snow and the Akitas, their tight-curled
Tails and massive shoulders, keep jumping
Into the snowbanks headfirst to find them,
Digging a tunnel in this snow thrown high,
Back to each paw print that gives them a sign of their kind.

III

CLASP

And you will come to me in sunlight
Where there is no sea,
Where all the rocks are broken,
Their jagged fingers
Touching us.

We will lie down before them.
We will lie down before them
Like crusts of wind
Our bodies the last hard thing left.

We were caught in their death step
You and I
As furious as wind,
As if our parents
Sat like Rumpelstiltskin
At the spinning wheel,
Weaving this net
That tangled us, then cast us out.

I will never go forward.
What is left is shadow, fade of flesh.
If you were here and reached out, your hand
Would pass through me, chilled.

Oh let me rage. Let me
Call down the stars all around
This, the start of my life sentence.
I pace each bar, shout your name.

Parasite

Grief is a second body
Come to sprout open your own
Starting in maybe your intestinal
Tract and expanding, up and out
Around your liver, which becomes
Puffier, takes on new life; then
Coiling up through your lungs
Threading its way through bronchioles
And alveoli so your lungs harden,
Can't open, and it is always
So difficult to breathe.

And then of course the heart,
The overwritten heart, which
Nonetheless responds physically
When inhabited like this,
The cortisol and epinephrine
Pushing it harder, faster,
In the middle of the night, gasping
For air and the nausea coiling
Up from the gut and the grief
Keeps reaching still:

Your throat tightens, it is as difficult
To swallow as to breathe and then
The final conquest, taking over
Your brain, either a fog so deep
You sit in the same corner for a week
Or the images keep rushing through
So fast they almost have a hand

Around your throat: your foot, his foot
Displacing leaves, the rustle,
The perfect stillness when you stopped
The pines deep arms of green

And yes, oh yes there was a bridge
Where you lay on your backs
Stared up at the sky and you want
It to stop, you want the fog back,
The fog is all you want.

What Takes Root

How do we outlast despair
Once it takes root like those
Climbing vines that spread up
The walls of houses, reach
Through rocks, tendrils spreading
In so many directions you
Have to cut them in several
Different places to even begin
To pull them back? Who owns
Despair, why do we listen to some
And not to others, why isn't it clearer
How much it shapes every single
Person's life: the man I train,
Helping him to take steps, drop
Down into a lunge, fighting
Against muscles bound up
By Parkinson's disease; my mother,
Grieving the death of her friend,
But he was the Hospital President,
A State Regent, Tucson Man of the Year
And no one knows him, no one remembers
Except a few of us old biddies scratching
Here in the corner and then no one will;
Or the way I walked up the driveway
That day, our first born in the NICU,
Me looking up to my neighbor's houses
And imagining them staring out at me
With my empty hands no baby in them
Thinking they must be thinking *that one*
Always was too weird to have a kid,

Moving outside of myself,
Following the body that shoulder-hunched
Itself up the driveway and then all that winter
Stood frozen at the kitchen sink, staring
Out at the birds and their flits of wings,
Repeating their names: *pine siskin.*
Red-breasted grosbeak. House finch.
Chickadee. Brown wren. Over and over
Until I could move again, the house
So quiet, the banks of snow so tall.

How to Bury Your First Born

Step 1:   Hallucinate his face in the driveway,
          As you back out the car.

Step 2:   Shut your mind against him,
          Clamp hard.

Step 3:   When you lose yourself staring at chickadees,
          Speak.

Step 4:   Give yourself up to him utterly, let him
          Right in. Invite him along with you,
          As if he'd made it to the point where he could walk.
          There he is, just down to your right—
          If you hold your hand out
          He will grab it. He never teethed.
          He had no first steps, and that wind,
          That wind conceives him.

Step 5:   Bid your girls look for him
          In the fourteenth day moon.
          Clasp them in your arms, then turn away.
          Bid them to watch him
          In every leaf. Bid them
          To rake each leaf slowly when it dies.

Step 6:   Understand this is a story
          You will be telling a long time.
          The milkweed pod
          Has spread its seed.
          Its top is thistle, milk-white.

Watching the River

The dead walk among us, unable
To let us know they still exist,
For they imagine they don't,
Observing each of us going about
Our daily lives, our fingers reaching
To touch each others' living faces,
To trace the shape of a nose bridge,
An eye, the cheek whose curve
Our fingertips have memorized,
Or the indentation just above a lip.
And they watch us, so hungry,
Reaching out, and think we do not
Feel them, think each day
They have been dead is a day
From which they are erased.

They do not know it is their lips
We trace when we touch,
Do not know they move through us
The way water moves
Past riverbanks, gathering,
Bringing with it the rush of roots,
Their substance stuck,
And we so unable to let them pass
To any other side.

Leave the Light On

For years, love was a long shadow
A dark smudge of hope
That would extend itself, then fade
Like charcoal smudged across paper.
But then there was your smile
Each time I looked up, your eyes
That looked directly into mine
Your hand always ready
To rest on my knee, your fingers
To entwine themselves with mine.
Love a long shadow, a dark smudge
Of hope, and you left the lights
On in your apartment
Because you knew it comforted me
When I drove up
Because you knew
I had just begun to bear
The beauty in the hollow of your throat.

TILT

On days like this the gray holds the branches
Of the trees down, air too heavy to stir,
Cold lowering the skies like a water tank
About to burst its rusty seams. I have seen
Pictures of you from when you were a boy,
Your eyes open, looking directly at the camera
With that kindness that is with you still,
Your quiet smile with your lips turned up
Slightly at the left corner, down at the right,
Your eyes so focused, bright, the same
From the time you were two, the same
Although your parents split and you moved
From place to place, first one stepmother,
Then another, then step-siblings and summers
With your mother, her head always resting
A little heavy on your shoulder, and you,
Your arm around her, your head
Tilted into hers. You love, and love,
And love, and love, and your eyes
Still haven't changed, not forty years
Later, my head resting on your chest
When you pull me in tight and cry out
Whenever I move in my sleep,
Holding me away from the gray.

WORLD PICTURES

(for Karen and Chelsea)

You turn toward the world and the world declines,
Other things on its mind like a man with a jaw
And a woman by his side, always the same man,
His fingers set, always the same girl, her body
Leaned into him, her shoulders lower than his,
And always, always their kids, their jaws, their eyes:
You turn toward the world and the world declines
Until she didn't, and after that, the same world,
Another picture bleeding in: the tops of your heads
Along the same lines, not one of you forward, one behind,
Your smiles turned toward each other, each other in your eyes
And the world looks on and smiles—it smiles—
It smiles this time, it does not decline.

CELLOS

My friends register
The day gay marriage
Is legalized, and they
Start planning the wedding
Two years before the event.

There are three bridal showers
For different groups of friends
And in all the Facebook photos
They wear white cotton sheaths
And even, in one photo, neck pearls.

At the shower I attend
There are the usual Crock Pots
And vases, and a food processor
From Williams-Sonoma.
They sit side by side, open them.

Such pretty girls. They do marathon training
To lose weight, post before and after pics,
The day of the wedding wear white gowns
With lace trains, bodices that sparkle
With beads. Their combat boots you can't see

But I know they are there, just as
I know what it feels like to long to
Come home safe, the glass of the windows
In place. Inside, the bamboo countertop
Will be clean. No one

Will yell at you, or hit.

THE TEA CART

All those summers of my childhood
The tea cart sat in the dining room,
A long room filled with light,
The cart's stately wheels and brass
A-glint with a vision of better things:

The carved glass-stoppered bottles,
Rich viscous liquids in ambers and whites,
The thin-stemmed champagne flutes
Like my grandmother's ballerina legs,
The shot glasses thick like my grandfather's chest.

My grandparents were beautiful like the glass
And their voices were always kind
And now the tea cart sits in my living room,
Sunlight twinkling across the long-necked bottles
And they are with me.

Words Making Worlds

There is so much noise even into
The middle of night I wake up
Just to listen to it stop:
Cars forever whispering
Along the parkway half a mile away,
The neighbor's children's screams and shrieks,
The endless hum of my own children's
Voices as they talk to stuffed
Owls or each other, words making
Worlds I can't see, the hum
Of the washing machine, hiss of water
Through the pipes, dogs growling and panting
In a whirling circle, teeth to tails
And worse: those horrible laugh tracks
On my children's TV, the mechanized
Music of computer games until
I pace from room to room yelling
"Quiet!" and they raise their hands
In glee, run from kitchen to living room,
Mocking me, pure noise pure love pure joy.

WHAT LIGHT IS

At the vet's office the student assistant
Helps me lift my Akita's stiff hips
So she can stand, ease her up for the X-ray
That will show the secrets of her lowering bones
So suddenly unsteady, the disjointed spine
That will not let her turn her head.

The student's name is Amy and she is pregnant
Like I am, though this is her first, and for me it's
My second, two-months close on the heels of the one
Who died, the one born with brain damage so bad
The MRI was just pockets of light like a cheesecloth
With too many holes sewn in, and Amy's hands

Reach out to steady me when my hands
Start to shake so I can't hold my dog up,
The way I try to keep my voice steady
As we discuss protocols and prognosis,
What mysterious force this could be
And my dog looks over at me

As she winces, a shiver of pain
Passing through her like a shock,
Her fur against my face and chest
As I struggle to stand in place.
We've been in this room for hours
It seems and the air ticks flat

While the voices of the other doctors rumble,
The clicks of machines while they diagnose and scan

And it's been too many machines for me,
The fear in my mouth a metal plate
Along with my heartbeat and my daughter's
And my dog's running fast against

My chest, so much steel and light and clean surface
And Amy holds her hands out, for this single moment
Her touch some steadiness I need,
Some skeleton against this skin of loss
Where the bodies of your loved ones
Breathe, then twitch, then fade.

Hair

One daughter's hair is sunlight, honey-blonde,
Its scent like wet straw. The other's is rockweed,
Slow-tangling vines. I brush each head each morning,
Try to smooth their strands into place, straighten
Tangles, untie the knots. One daughter
Wants her hair to fall around her ears
(they stick out too far she says), the other wants
Multiple braids mixed with ponytails, three on one side,
Two the other, all three of us with hair so fine
It feels like cotton or butterfly eggs and the long slide of fibers
Are like spider webs bouncing back in my hands,
My own hair thinning, more strands falling out
Every marathon I run, every carbohydrate
I can't bring myself to eat as if I've begun
To give myself up, pieces of me
Falling off but rejoining in them
Fibers that are starting to unweave.

NOISE

Quiet, quiet! my daughters say, rolling their eyes,
Extending their arms to the sky, laughing
In imitation of me. They scamper across
The living room floor, their noise
Concatenation, joy, something so different
Than my mother's voice, the one whose tones
I can't stop hearing, not words but tones
Like a blue jay's screech, enough to tear
The tender folds, Eustachian tubes
Folding up the inner ear until there
Is nothing left, just a teetering over vertigo
So I can choke back those tones in my own voice,
Keep my daughters from feeling each noise
Like a shock, folding into themselves
Like shed feathers, as if each of their words
Was extra, not gathering their bones
And teeth and nerves and shrieks
Instead into this, my daily light.

For Art

In the picture from the elementary school
Art exhibit, my daughter stands
By her painting in a fake leopard fur coat,
Her face lit up like the colors
Behind her, the careful wash
Of red for skin. The coat's
Sleeves drag long for she's too young
For this fur at five, too eager
To flash alone against this sea
Of lights gleaming against the glass
Of other children's works. "I'm
the only kindergartener they picked,"
she was saying the moment the flashbulb flicked.

Last night at the graduate party,
She brought her blue guitar to play,
Expecting all noise to stop, all eyes to
Turn to her, her voice like some medieval
Shepherd calling her flock to attention,
Each note soaked with magic
Much bigger than her coat.

When the noise of the party rolls over her
In waves, what seems to her a million voices abuzz
With their own concerns, the light in her face fades
And she collapses in my lap to weep. I rub
My hand along her back and think of the essay
I'd read that morning by a poet who claimed
The writing as we've known it is done,
With so many voices, so much writing

Covering every possible niche so that
All there is left to us is to cut and paste and that way
Join the frantic conversation with the rest.
The individual writer is dead he said, the painters
Knew this in the 1920s, and writers so behind the curve
Will waste their lives trying to make themselves
Stand out. I think of my daughter
In her leopard coat, her smile in tandem
With the camera's flash,
And long to tell her we must do this
Regardless, we creatures of longing,
We clichés of flashing words, leopard coats.

Baby Teeth

My daughter's baby teeth have fallen out
And grown back with multiple gaps between,
Matching her Little Orphan Annie freckles
Matching the way she throws her arms
Behind to meet her legs on the gymnastics beam,
Flipping through air so fast
She becomes a blur I can't see.

She points her toes and fingers, nods
Her head to bended knee at the sections
Of her routine when she must stop
Spinning, stand still in an instant of grace
And she does, her jaw set, her eyes
Fixed on a spot to the front of her
Fierce as cigarette burns.

She's eight and she practices
Five hours a day, each leg-lowering
Pistol on a beam, each bar kip
She needs to fly over as accessible
As her lungs, rotating through motions
Out and in. But lately they're learning
Some movements she can't get yet:
Double-back handsprings and multiple
Front flips that come easily to Charli,
Her best friend.

How do we learn such grace,
What happens when our limitations find us
Like they do as certain as there will be wind,

Why does it always make us cry,
Like she does, grinding the gaps
Between her teeth, shaking her fists,
Throwing herself to the ground as if
Her failure to fly will leave her stranded here,

A girl, suddenly this strange thing
Of slumped shoulders, the shame
Of feeling for the first time she is
Ordinary, just a girl.

Never Won Anything

My oldest daughter brings her science papers
Home that have the highest scores,
We don't see the rest. We don't know
Until the report card comes
She has been doing this,
Holding her lower scores inside,
Probing them like a rotten tooth,
Waiting for it to fall out.
She knows what numbers mean to me
And wants me to smile when I ask her
How she's doing in school, my frowns
Or the edge in my voice
Make her shoulders slump forward,
Drop her head.
It's not the grades themselves
She cares about, a 79 or an 86
Sliding over her like rain
Sliding down her parka's hood,
The hood she'll keep drawn over
Her head unless you ask her
Several times to put it down
And she looks out from it
Onto a world I can't imagine,
A world I struggle to read
With her mind and come up blank
The way my refuge of perfect grades
And letters is blankness to her.
This daughter has never won anything,

Always kicked the soccer ball down the field
The wrong way when she was five,
Struggled to make any sense from letters
When she was six, dyslexia twisting her
Words like a macramé bracelet gone wrong.

She loves folding origami, the careful lines
Each flip of paper makes, but her balance
In gymnastics always found her hips
Skewed to the wrong side, her back arched
When it should be straight.
While her sister wins art contests, comes in first
In every race, brings home report cards
With perfect lines of A's, this daughter
Never wins anything, just shocks me sometimes
With the sheer intelligence of something
She has said about the ways people
Treat each other without kindness, how
They act in ways that can be nothing but wrong,
And this daughter has never won anything,
Never won anything, except my love.

A Bowl. A Wine Glass. Plate.

My partner and I look confusedly around as we begin
To decide what to take from my father's house,
How best to clean it out. My step into
The living room makes me draw my breath in,
For the first thing I see is an old University
Of Arizona cross-country poster of me, thirty
Years old now, framed and centered. I look from it
To the paintings of Canadian geese
Launching over a lake, and Jerry starts to tell me
How exactly my father died. Jerry is
My father's landlord, but from the way he talks
About him, I know he was also my father's friend.

I knew something was wrong when I saw
He hadn't gotten his paper and he hadn't
Fed his birds. Fed those birds every morning.
So I knocked on the door and said John!
John! But he couldn't hear me so I went in.
He was on the floor. Jerry, he says to me,
I'm going to need a little help. And he can't
Move at all and I had a time of it, I'm telling
You, because John wasn't a small man.
I told him I'd have to take him to the hospital
And he didn't want to go. John, I tell him,
I have to take you. You're not going to die
On my watch.

Take all the time you need Jerry says
And leaves the house, and I sit at my father's
Desk going through datebooks and check

Book receipts and taking it all,
Packing his watches into cardboard boxes
And the kitchen is last, his last plate and fork
Still sitting on the drainboard and I take that too,
And the wineglass that, because it is yellower
Than the others, I assume he used the most.

That night I howl with grief that sounds
Like nothing I've ever heard, some wild
Thing like a Rottweiler growling mixed
With the sound of shearing metal,
The way it pulls and twists and finally rips.
It's early April and Mirror Lake is still frozen,
Pure white outside the balcony of the Golden
Arrow Lakeside Resort and my partner
Sits beside me forehead against my back
And feels me shake.
I don't know how long I go on like this
But I scream and scream until my voice
Feels clear, my head empty.

Where Light Falls

We didn't have a funeral for my father.
Instead, his landlord, Jerry, also the funeral
Director in his town of Keene Valley, NY,
Population 1,105, had collected
The rest of the ashes he hadn't given to me, placed them
In my father's favorite Native American pot,
And scouted out somewhere to scatter them.
He knew where my father had hiked with his dogs
In the years he could still walk, and he asked
The owners of the land if he could scatter my father
In a place where his steps had traced the ground
So many times those years earlier. When they said yes,
Jerry found what he told us
Was exactly the right place—a tiny clearing
Off to the side of the path near a stream,
A place, he explained to me,
Where the light falls all day,
Bright shaft through the canopy of trees.
He said he'd come back at different times
To test it, to see if the light was still there
At 8 a.m., and noon, and 4 p.m., and later . . .
I wanted him to have a little light,
Jerry tells me. *I can do that for him anyhow.*

So my daughters and my ex
And my partner at the time pile into Jerry's
Ford F-150 extra cab and we all fit, the girls
And I in front, my partner and my ex in back
And drive up the steep, unpaved mountain road
Where you can't see the houses from the street

And we pull off on a shallow embankment
And walk together the rest of the way, this
Unlikely funeral procession, the girls and I
Pulling ahead so that Jerry yells up to us
If you get to the river you've gone too far.
I don't know what he thinks about the lot of us—
He looked at us all hard once but didn't say
A thing. I bring a locket I made with my father's
Picture tucked in, a miniature of him riding
His Scorpion snowmobile sometime in the late
1960s, its black frame launched through the air
Over a heavy embankment of snow so my father
Is caught there, mid-air, our dog running
Behind almost out of the frame but with his
Front legs flying up just the same as the machine
And my father and my dog launch there
And hold and I wrap the chain of the locket
Around the black and tan painted clay pot,
As Jerry and I scatter some ashes in all
The spaces there is light and I place
The locket face-up in the brightest spot
Between some roots where the rough bark
Will hold it. Nobody knows what to say,

The girls to the side throwing fragments of leaves
Into the stream, my ex and my partner taking pictures,
Trying to capture the ashes in the light,
And Jerry and I trying to say words about my father
That would stick. All I can say is *he was amazing,*
He wasn't what people would think, and Jerry says

I know and *I reckon I've done right by him now,*
I promised him I'd find him a place and we all know
It's time to go but we walk around a bit first to try
To memorize where we are, the roar of the river
In front of us and the dead quiet of the mountain
Behind. It's 11 a.m. on a Sunday, June 8, 2014,
What would have been his birthday—another touch
Jerry insisted upon—and together we all bow
Our heads and turn, my family and this stranger
Who cared for my father, picked him up off the floor
And brought him to the hospital that final time,
Who knew to call me—me, not my mother,
Not my sister, when he finally died.

This time, unlike in April when we cleaned out
The house, I don't cry. I hold my partner's hand,
Look around me, and try to remember Jerry's
Place where the light falls a certain way between
The trees and holds my father safe.

Caelan at Thirteen

After years of being so much smaller
Than me, years of fitting easily
Into my lap, as if overnight
My daughter is taller than I am,
Starts wearing my shoes.

This is a relief since now at least
I have some further, less selfish
Reason for buying them, all
Those nearly identical pairs
Of Frye boots, but what I notice
Most is how well she wears them,
How, on her, they are transformed
Into lines of art, a startling grace.

She wears her hair long, and so curly
When the humidity hits, with chin-length
Bangs that are always
Covering part of her face. When
She sits next to me, I try
To push the bangs aside,
But she just puts them back,
And smiles, her blue Warby Parker
Glasses her "hipster nerd badge,"
She tells me. Her legs have filled out
To look just like mine, but her face,
Heart-shaped, her chin at the right angle
And her huge bright blue eyes,
Has only small echoes of mine
With its too-small eyes
And too-big nose that juts out.

There is a magic in the way
She moves her hands, a grace of fingers,
And the way she smiles and speaks.
How did this perfect creature come from me,
How did she end up this strong,
This generous, this whole, I am thinking
As I listen to her tell me how she
Is the counselor for all of her friends,
How she's the only one that can calm them,
My daughter, at thirteen, this unicorn, all legs
And brains and speed, now winning
All her cross-country meets and reassuring
Herself when she too melts down,
Caelan, it's only hormones, what
You are feeling isn't real.
My daughter, who knows at thirteen
Things it has taken me at least
Four decades to start sorting out,
What her grandmother, my father's mother Annie,
Could never sort through with all those
Emotions running through her like flame,
Making her dangerous, the one you can't stand
To be around; never for Annie, four decades for me,
What my daughter knows now
At thirteen.

BIOGRAPHICAL NOTE

Leslie Heywood is Professor of English and Creative Writing at SUNY-Binghamton and author of several books of nonfiction including *Pretty Good for a Girl* (The Free Press / Simon & Schuster, 1999). Published widely, her poetry has been nominated twice for a Pushcart Prize.